CONTENTS

KU-524-598

CHAPTER 1

PUSHING THE LIMITS OF TECHNOLOGY

A surfer parks her car at the beach. She takes a small plastic drone from the back seat. She attaches a **high-definition** video camera to the bottom. Then she straps a flight-control device that looks like a watch onto her wrist. She places the drone onto the sand, and then paddles out into the frothy ocean waves. Once she catches a good wave, she presses a button on the controller. The drone lifts off the sand and zips out towards her. It follows her as she rides the wave, catching all of the action around her. It zooms in and out to show all the angles of her ride. As her ride ends, the drone flies back to its original position on the sand. The new drone worked perfectly. Her test of the drone is finished. She will give the drone manufacturer feedback on the drone's performance. She also now has the ultimate "selfie" video.

Extreme sports athletes aren't the only people who are trying out drones. Military forces, delivery companies and **meteorologists** are all experimenting with them. Although thousands of drones are in use, the ones being tested now are pushing the limits of what drones can do.

Many drone manufacturers focus on a drone's ability to take high-quality video and photographs. Cameras can either be built-in or attached to a drone.

high-definition having a high clarity of visual presentation; cameras labelled as high definition meet a certain resolution standard and requirements

meteorologist person who studies and predicts the weather

CHAPTER 2

THE INS AND OUTS OF DRONES

What is a drone? Some people think of drones only as aerial vehicles. But they are much more than that. Drones that fly in the air are sometimes called unmanned aerial vehicles (UAVs). But some drones can be used underwater. People usually operate drones using remote control devices. Some drones can also fly by themselves on a preset flight path. Once the flight path is set, a **Global Positioning System** (GPS) guides the drone.

Drones with four rotors are often called quadcopters.

Generally, a person is not on board a drone. But drones can carry people as passengers. The vehicle is still considered a drone if the person on board has no power to control the vehicle.

Drones come in many shapes and sizes. Military drones at sea often look like submarines. Fixed-wing UAVs look like **gliders**. Rotary UAVs resemble helicopters. Many **rotor** drones have four rotors, but some have eight or more. Some small UAVs can carry items such as books and medical supplies. Large military UAVs can carry big cameras and weapons for combat. Some of these UAVs weigh more than 1,815 kilograms (4,000 pounds) when empty.

Global Positioning System electronic tool used to find the location of an object; this system uses signals from satellites

glider lightweight aircraft that flies by floating and rising on air currents instead of by engine power

rotor set of rotating blades that lifts an aircraft off the ground

RECHARGING AND REFUELLING

Drones have limited flight times. When their battery power or fuel runs out, they need to be recharged or refuelled. Large military drones use fuel to fly. Many small drones land on a drone port on rooftops or the ground to recharge their batteries. Some researchers are looking for ways to increase flight times for drones. In 2014, a student at the Massachusetts Institute of Technology (MIT) came up with a possible way to recharge small drones using power lines. Drones would perch on a power line to recharge their batteries.

In 2016, aircraft manufacturer Boeing was granted a **patent** for a mid-air recharging system. The drone would have a cord called a tether. The tether could drop down and attach to a drone power station on the ground. The drone could stay in the air to be recharged instead of landing.

patent legal document giving someone sole rights to make or sell a product

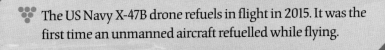

The US Navy X-47B drone refuels in flight in 2015. It was the first time an unmanned aircraft refuelled while flying.

OMEGA TANKER

Boeing also designs sea drones. In 2016, Boeing built *Echo Voyager*. This drone submarine can dive to 3,353 metres (11,000 feet) below the surface of the water. It can stay underwater for at least six months. It has a **hybrid** electric-fuel system that allows it to recharge underwater. Unlike most other sea drones, it doesn't need to return to a surface ship to recharge. After testing, Boeing hopes to make these drones available for companies to buy.

hybrid mix of two different types; hybrid engines run on electricity and petrol or diesel fuel

CHAPTER 3

MILITARY AND SPACE EXPERIMENTAL DRONES

The United States, the United Kingdom, China, Israel and many other countries use military drones. Military drones help to keep members of the armed forces out of harm's way. Many armed forces partner with manufacturers to design and test drones. If testing goes well, the armed forces may buy the drones. Some drone manufacturers also sell drones directly to armed forces.

WEAVING AROUND OBSTACLES

In January 2016, the Defense Advanced Research Projects Agency (DARPA) in the United States completed its first flight test on a drone. The small, lightweight drone is about the size of a seagull. It carries a camera, **sonar** and **lidar**. This equipment helps the drone fly into destroyed buildings filled with debris without crashing. It can travel at 72 kilometres (45 miles) per hour while weaving in and out of obstacles. The US military would like to one day use this drone to search inside unstable buildings to help to keep soldiers safe.

The DARPA drone's small size would allow it to fit through windows.

sonar device that uses sound waves to find objects; sonar stands for sound navigation and ranging

lidar device that measures the distance to an object by bouncing laser light off the object and timing how long it takes the light to return; lidar stands for light detection and ranging

SR-72 DRONE

Skunk Works is the advanced development programme of aircraft manufacturer Lockheed Martin. Skunk Works built aircraft such as the US military SR-71 Blackbird spy plane. The SR-71 was the fastest plane to have ever flown. All Skunk Works programmes are important to US national security, and they are secret. But future Skunk Works drones are likely to have more **stealth** technology.

The Skunk Works SR-72 Blackbird drone is planned to be finished in 2030. Lockheed plans for the drone to fly at more than 6,437 kilometres (4,000 miles) per hour. This is six times the speed of sound! Developers want it to fly undetected, take photos and get to any location on Earth in about an hour.

an artist's drawing of the SR-72

TARANIS

Aircraft manufacturer BAE Systems built the Taranis for the British armed forces in 2010. Since then, it has completed several successful tests. The stealth drone is meant to be invisible to **radar**. The drone can travel at more than 1,127 kilometres (700 miles) per hour. The British military plans to use the test results to develop future drones and fighter planes. Some experts consider it the most advanced aircraft ever made in the United Kingdom.

DIVINE EAGLE

The Chinese government has recently increased its military spending. The Divine Eagle is a large **prototype** drone. It is meant to defend China's airspace and hunt enemy aircraft carriers in oceans. It has several radars to help to find enemy aircraft, ships or ground targets. The radars can detect objects on any side of the drone.

stealth having the ability to move without being seen by radar

radar device that uses radio waves to track the location of objects

prototype the first version of an invention that tests an idea to see if it will work

A TOP-SECRET SPACE PLANE

For the Boeing X-37B space drone, the skies are not the limit. The X-37B rides a rocket all the way to space. It is a joint project between the National Aeronautics and Space Administration (NASA) and the US Air Force. The unmanned spacecraft is 8.8 metres (29 feet) long and has a wingspan of 4.6 metres (15 feet). Once in **orbit**, the X-37B flies on a preset flight path. Since its missions are top secret, little information about what the drone does is made public. Air Force officials say it is used to develop reusable spacecraft technologies and to conduct experiments.

A FUTURE HELPER FOR ASTRONAUTS

What might be the easiest way to get a snack aboard the International Space Station (ISS) in the future? Send the drone! The ArachnoBeeA drone is designed to navigate inside the ISS. It is like a combination of an aerial drone and a ground robot. The drone can fly around the space station and bring items to astronauts. It also has limbs so that it can attach itself to the walls of the ISS and crawl from place to place. It has a mechanical arm that it uses to grab objects while crawling.

The X-37B taxis at the Astrotech space operations facility in Florida in 2010.

FACT

On its first launch in 2010, the X-37B became the first US spacecraft to land on a runway under its own control.

 orbit path an object follows while circling another object in space

A DRONE BARGE

Space rockets require an enormous amount of energy to get into space. They have powerful engines and carry a lot of fuel. Rockets are made up of stages called boosters. Each booster is a separate part of the rocket. After the rocket is launched, the boosters separate from the rocket. The first booster separates first. Then a specific amount of time later, the second booster separates. Both boosters usually drop into the ocean. They are only sometimes retrieved by ship crews.

On 8 April 2016, a Falcon 9 rocket launched from Kennedy Space Center in Cape Canaveral, Florida, USA. But when the first booster broke off, it didn't drop into the water. Instead it landed on a drone ship that was floating in the Atlantic Ocean. The booster can now be reused for another rocket launch.

The drone ship's name is *Of Course I Still Love You*. The huge drone is about the same size as a football field. It is 91 metres (300 feet) long and 52 metres (170 feet) wide. Operators can control the barge with remote control to get it in the location needed to catch the booster. Its guidance system can also be preset.

FACT

The barge *Of Course I Still Love You* is named after a ship in Iain M. Banks' science fiction book *The Player of Games*.

A rocket stage lands successfully on the deck of *Of Course I Still Love You* in 2016.

CHAPTER 4

DELIVERY AND HUMANITARIAN EXPERIMENTAL DRONES

Imagine you're at home and hungry. You grab your computer, go online and bring up the website of your favourite pizza place. You place your order. Twenty minutes later, your wait is over. A drone is hovering over your doorstep, and it drops a fresh pizza into your hands. Could drone delivery be common one day? Some experts think so. But there's still a lot of work that needs to be done before that can happen.

In 2013, delivery company Deutsche Post tested deliveries of medicine using a drone in Germany.

Around the world people have experimented with using drones for delivery services. Businesses in the United Kingdom have tested a variety of delivery drones. In 2013, a London restaurant used drones to deliver sushi to customers at their tables. The same year, a drone delivered pizza in a test flight near London.

The German delivery company DHL conducted test flights with delivery drones called "parcelcopters" in 2014. The drones delivered medicines and other supplies to a remote island in the North Sea called Juist. The drones were some of the first European drones to be sent on a job outside the operator's field of vision. However, operators on the ground were able to see where the drones were going using their on-board cameras.

HUMANITARIAN DRONES

In Africa, companies are testing drones to see if they can deliver food, medicine and other important supplies to rural areas. In sub-Saharan Africa, many of the roads are not passable during the rainy season. This problem prevents many people from receiving needed supplies.

A company called Matternet is working with humanitarian organization UNICEF to test drones in Malawi. In 2016, Matternet's test drone left a health clinic. It flew 9.7 kilometres (6 miles) to a hospital. The drone carried fake blood samples. In the future, Matternet hopes to carry real blood samples from newborn babies. The samples will need to be tested to see if the infants were born with **HIV**. Normally, the samples would be taken by motorcycle. This form of delivery is slow and expensive. A drone delivery system could be less costly and faster.

 HIV virus that causes an immune system disease called AIDS; HIV stands for human immunodeficiency virus

Matternet also hopes to one day use drones to deliver goods to people all over the world. It could let a person be both a sender and a receiver. For example, a person living in a rural village could receive goods from urban areas. Then the same person could load up the drone with home-made goods to be sold at an urban market.

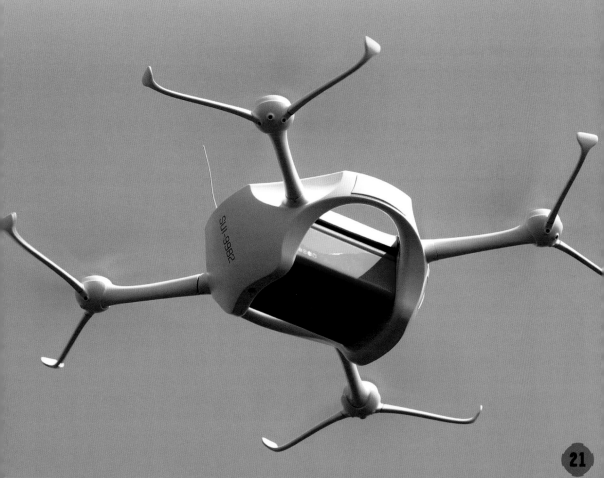

A Matternet drone flies during a presentation in Switzerland in 2015.

VIEWS FROM THE SKY

The United Nations (UN) and aid organizations use drones to learn more about people's needs. Drones surveyed disaster areas after the Haiti earthquakes in 2010 and the Balkan floods of south-eastern Europe in 2014. The views from the sky were especially important to help to send humanitarian aid. When a disaster happens, aerial images show exactly what is going on in the area. They show where the damage is and where the most help is needed.

Aerial images from drones can also show other types of crises. In 2016, drones surveyed the size of **refugee** camps in Syria. This information helped aid organizations learn how to best help the refugees.

FACT

California company Zipline has developed small fixed-wing drones. The company hopes to use the drones to deliver medical supplies in Rwanda. The drones are expected to increase the speed of delivery from weeks or months to just hours.

 refugee person who has to leave a place to escape war or other disasters

A rescue drone flies in Lebanon in 2015. It is designed to find people who are drowning and throw a lifebelt to them.

CHAPTER 5

EXPERIMENTAL RECREATIONAL DRONES

The possibility of making life-saving medical deliveries shows the serious side of drones. But drones have a fun side too. People of all ages like playing with drones. Some people even come up with new uses for drones as they experiment.

 A drone takes photographs while shooting a film in India in 2012.

DRONES ON STAGE

In 2014, a fleet of 15 drones flew during a concert in London's Barbican theatre. The drones were costumed and lit with spotlights. They flew over the audience as an orchestra performed music on stage. The drones moved in time with the music. The producer of the event compared the coordination to that of a military operation.

The entertainment industry uses drones to make films, stage plays and concerts more exciting for audiences. Film-makers like to get close-up action shots of stunts for their films. To get an overhead shot, directors can use helicopters. But helicopters can be very expensive. They must also stay far away from the set for the safety of the people on the ground. Drones have resolved both of these issues. They're much less expensive than helicopters and they can get very close to the action on set. Many people in the film industry feel that drones will continue to become more valuable to film-making.

PERSONAL FLYING MACHINE

Would you take a ride on a drone? Chinese company Ehang has invented a drone that can carry a human passenger. The Ehang 184 drone looks like a small helicopter. It has four arms. Each arm has a rotor attached to its top and underside. The Ehang 184 is designed to carry a person weighing up to 120 kilograms (264 pounds).

Ehang 184 would allow people to travel short distances in the air. You would just hop on board and program in where you want to go. The drone would then transport you to your destination. Don't expect a long flight, though. The drone can only stay in the air for about 20 minutes before needing to be recharged.

The Ehang 184 was displayed at the 2016 Consumer Electronics Show in Las Vegas, in the United States.

FACT

The "184" in the name Ehang 184 was given because the drone has one passenger, eight propellers and four arms.

CHAPTER 6

THE FUTURE OF DRONES

The possibilities for drone use in the future are very exciting. Drone technology will continue to develop, which could lead to even more ideas. For example, today meteorologists are using aerial drones to learn more about severe weather. They fly drones into hurricanes and thunderstorms. The drones can then measure wind speed, air temperature and other meteorological factors. In the future, drones may help scientists to understand why tornadoes form, which is not fully understood today. From drones with facial recognition software to drones with **hypersonic** speed, researchers are hard at work exploring drone capabilities.

NEW RULES FOR DRONES

Major increases in drone use are expected worldwide by 2020. With this increase, some people worry that drones could cause problems without more laws. Many countries have laws about drone use. In the United Kingdom, the Civil Aviation Authority (CAA) makes drone laws. Local laws may also govern drone use. Many laws focus on safety. Pilots and passengers of other aircraft need to be protected from collisions with drones. People and animals on the ground must be kept safe from crashing drones. Because many drones have cameras, personal privacy concerns also have to be considered. With laws in place, drone enthusiasts can enjoy their hobby and keep themselves and others safe.

hypersonic relating to a speed five or more times that of sound in air

GLOSSARY

glider lightweight aircraft that flies by floating and rising on air currents instead of by engine power

Global Positioning System electronic tool used to find the location of an object; this system uses signals from satellites

high-definition having a high clarity of visual presentation

HIV virus that causes an immune system disease called AIDS; HIV stands for human immunodeficiency virus

hybrid mix of two different types

hypersonic relating to a speed five or more times that of sound in air

lidar device that measures the distance to an object by bouncing laser light off the object and timing how long it takes the light to return; lidar stands for light detection and ranging

meteorologist person who studies and predicts the weather

orbit path an object follows while circling another object in space

patent legal document giving someone sole rights to make or sell a product

prototype first version of an invention that tests an idea to see if it will work

radar device that uses radio waves to track the location of objects

refugee person who has to leave a place to escape war or other disasters

rotor set of rotating blades that lifts an aircraft off the ground

sonar device that uses sound waves to find objects; sonar stands for sound navigation and ranging

stealth having the ability to move without being seen by radar

READ MORE

Drones (Beginners Plus), Henry Brook (Usborne Publishing, 2016)

Drones, Martin J. Dougherty (Scholastic, 2014)

The Complete Guide to Drones, Adam Juniper (Ilex Press, 2015)

WEBSITES

www.bbsrc.ac.uk/news/research-technologies/2015/150929-f-octocopter-experimen-tal-drone-agricultural-research
This site has news and video about an experimental drone being used for agricultural research.

www.caa.co.uk/droneaware
Check out the Civil Aviation Authority website for drone laws and safety guides.

INDEX